PEOPLE POWERED

TIPS AND INSPIRATION
TO BUILDING STRONG
BUSINESS RELATIONSHIPS

FRANK DAPPAH

Copyright © 2012 Ostrich press

All rights reserved.

ISBN: 9798742845836

PEOPLE-POWERED

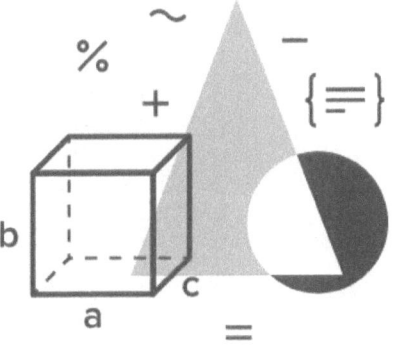

OSTRICH

CONTENTS

0	A Note to you, the reader	09
1	Friend of a friend	15
2	Self-talk	22
3	Communion	28
4	Labels	32
5	Haters and fools	36
6	Glass houses	43
7	Corporate courtship	50
8	Brand equity	55
9	It's complicated	67
10	Marriage boot camp	73
11	Moving targets	80
12	Growing pains	88

14	Corner offices	106
15	Clan adhocracy	112
16	Community equity	119
17	It Takes a village	128
18	Thank you	135
19	About the author	144

People-powered

A Note to You, the Reader

As a small business owner and entrepreneur, I have been blessed to be able to make a living based on the income earned from doing what I love the most: Building my business and investing in others. Along this wonderful journey that is my (young) life, I have had the pleasure of being in the presence of many truly inspiring people, both young and seasoned.

The work I have done, since the age of 27, when I left the corporate world to pursue my dream of being an entrepreneur - for better or worse - has exposed me to many different experiences, opportunities, and failures.

In this book, as I often do, I will share outcomes of investment/business growth and/or acquisition strategies, tips, insights, and advice.

Though most of these may have resulted in not-so-bad, or good outcomes, others have resulted in substantially adverse consequences.

With that in mind, I want to be clear that I am not a licensed business coach, financial professional, or legal strategist.

I am merely a student and observer of the business world. And while I am more than happy to share what I have learned from my experiences, none of the information I share with you is intended, nor should be construed, to be professional financial or business advice.

If you need help in these areas, consult area-specific professionals.

Neither I nor my publisher is responsible for anything that happens in your own professional and/or business life - good or bad- as a result of doing what I advise in this book.

In fact, these are just my thoughts and experiences and should be treated as such.

> Good luck
> Frank

People-powered

People rarely succeed unless they have fun in what they are doing.

-Dale Carnegie

People-powered

CHAPTER 1

FRIEND OF A FRIEND

Dale Carnegie, the famous inventor, writer, and all-around forward-thinking human, once said that above all else, the key to success is learning how to manage one's relationships with others successfully.

He would even admit that he wished that he had been much better at conducting himself in ways that avoided unnecessary conflict with others- especially in business.

I, too, have read what I consider to be his best work: "How to Win Friends and Influence People". To me, this is life's skeleton key. Far too often, folks like you and I believe that in business, success is a path that only involves, well, success.

Winning awards, making tons of cash, and so on. The thing that wiser folks know is that success is not the key to life. Happiness is. And for many of us, especially as we age, we are happy when we have had some success in life - among other things like good health, fewer regrets, and so on.

Success then becomes the path to happiness and not the other way around. Once we add on the fact that we only get one shot at life, therefore we only get one shot at success, happiness becomes one of life's most sought-after, and fleeting luxuries. One to be pursued vociferously.

So, the quest in life, at least in our younger years, is to define what success means to us. To some, success is having their own profitable company, with tons of cash in the bank, a nice car, and a fancy house.

Others are happy to have a great job,

great friends, and a healthy happy family.

It is not my place to aid anyone in the definition of their version of happiness and success.

Hell, some spend most of their lives looking for that spark. That warm and fuzzy feeling. That state of being that helps you shed all (or at least, most) of the adverse feelings, consequences, and occurrences that come with feeling trapped in a dream deferred.

And make no mistake about it. "Everybody's looking for that something. One thing that makes it all complete". As Ruben Studdard so passionately sings in his debut single, "Flying without wings".

Circle of success

One of the most important lessons I have come to learn about life is that it is about people. No, for real. No matter how successful you become, from a financial standpoint, you will undoubtedly find it difficult to enjoy the fruits of your labor, or life for that matter, if you have no other humans to share said fruits and/or life with.

Even if you are one of those obnoxious types who loves to flaunt their successes on social media, you must admit that others seeing you accomplish your goals brings you some sort of satisfaction.

Whether it is feelings of superiority, the expectation of some sort of envy, or whatever you are into, the key ingredient in you getting to feel good about yourself still depends on others/other people, right?

Others seeing what you got going on. Others being jealous of you. Even in this context, you still need others.

Of course, I like to advocate for far healthier ways to extract satisfaction out of life, but you get my point, don't you?

Regardless of the road you take to find your special something, you need others in your life.

The most miserable people in life are those without others. Those that – for one reason or another – find themselves by themselves. Alone in this often-cruel world.

Business relationships
Tackling the issue of happiness and success in life is a big topic. I will be the first to admit that.

Certainly, one that cannot be fully addressed in one little book. I will not attempt such an awesome feat. Rather, I want us to address the ways in which folks like you and I: Entrepreneurs, can effectively manage our relationships with the people we do business with. In such a way that not only allows for success in our commercial ventures, but also clears the proverbial runway for our overall success and happiness to take off.

In the next few chapters, I shall try to do just that.

I shall try to attempt to shares with you, the various techniques I have used in the past (and still use) to try to cultivate and nurture healthy business relationships.

People-powered

CHAPTER 2

SELF-TALK

I guess, looking back now, I have always been an entrepreneur at heart. Even before I knew what the term was, or meant, I wanted to grow up to work for myself. Like most kids that grew up to be self-employed, I did the typical things.

I had many little Side Hustles going all the way back to grade school. For me, there was no other way to earn a living. I guess, for better or worse, you could blame my folks for setting me up this way.

Born this way.
You see, growing up, mom and dad were

business folk. What made my experience being raised by those two so unique is that not only were they entrepreneurs, but they were also business partners.

In fact, according to legend, they were in business together, way before they were in love, and got married. I have never been able to confirm this version of the story though.

My childhood dinner table - although we weren't the "eat together" type of family - was always full of talk about "the business". That is all my parents ever talked about: Their 50 plus employee silverware-making company they had literally started in our backyard.

My folks worked from home. Except, our house was always full of people. Between the personal staff and the guys and gals in the backyard, plus the support staff, not to mention the customers, my home -

growing up was always filled with people. To this day, I have to remind my wife that I pretty much grew up on an industrial site.

Rate of change of momentum

Of course, I did not know it then, but these unique circumstances would forever shape the way I looked at work, business, my relationship with others (in business), money, how I spend my time, and so on.

It also helped greatly that I understood what made my folks' personal and business relationship work so well.

For one, they both possessed skills that were of great value to the business. More importantly, they both valued the skills each of them brought to the table and leaned on each other to fill the gap in their respective toolkits.

The old block

My father, like me, is a tinkerer. An

inventor of sorts. As far back as I can remember, his thing was taking things apart to see how they worked and trying to reverse-engineer almost everything he could get his hands on. From our toys to major household appliances, and the hardware at the factory, nothing in his path was safe.

He was also very extreme and fully committed to whatever he decided to do. I am this way too. I go all-in on everything I do. I cannot help it. It is who I am.

My mother's child

My momma, on the other hand, is a true Ashanti: A bean counter for real. A trader. A saleswoman.

I definitely got some of my mom's personality in me. I love sales and selling stuff.

While others shy away from talking

to total strangers about this or that idea, I love it. In fact, I would much rather spend my time doing "business stuff" than anything else.

I love interacting with folks in most commercial capacities. I love talking to customers to get a sense of what their needs are, and to get valuable feedback on the many ways in which we, as a company, can improve upon our products and services.

I love talking to other entrepreneurs, especially younger ones as I have come to realize that there is so much on old guy like me can learn from those who are young enough to be at the forefront of innovation.

People-powered

CHAPTER 3

COMMUNION

With this kind of early childhood training, I would of course grow up to be an entrepreneur. I left the workforce at the tender age of 27 to go start my own business. I rented my very first office space in the queen city, and I haven't looked back since. Well, maybe I did a few times.

My path, I must say, has been a mixed bag. I have had some success in business and in my personal life. As I get older, I realize that though both go hand-in-hand, as I was saying earlier, one's definition of success determines one's benchmark for happiness.

Without relitigating the point, it helps to consider the theory that how happy you are greatly relies on how closely matched (at any giving time) your definition, and expectation of success are to your current situation.

This is true for most of us. Though different groups of people define personal success differently, according to a recent Gallup poll, folks with household incomes of over $200k scored highest (72 out of 100) when asked to rate how successful they believed they are.

And consider the fact that among those in the U.S making over $250k a year, over 70% of them are in business for themselves.

It is plain to see, given these set of facts, that if we are to tie our personal definition of success to our state of happiness. And our success depends greatly on not just how much we make, but being in business, then it is clear as day, that one of the main ways to reach our personal happiness/success goals is to go into business for ourselves.

Which, in all fairness, most of us do, or try to, anyway. Do we always hit the mark though? Not even close.

People-powered

CHAPTER 4

LABELS

I am sure you know that the rate of failure in business is remarkably high. With all the guys and gals jumping into the realm of self-employment every year, survey says, over time, less than 5% of us will make it.

Meaning, most of us will fail at what we are doing for one reason or another. Truth be told, your business or my business can fail for a number of reasons.

From lack of adequate funding, to mismatched Product/market fit, businesses fail all the time.

I can bear witness to this harsh reality. I would start several companies till I found one that worked.

So, as I approach my forties, I find myself more interested in helping other entrepreneurs with what little I have learned in the most specific areas of business.

My wife - who is also my business partner - and I started a private investment firm with hopes of finding other entrepreneurs/startups - mostly black and brown folks- to invest in.

Along this new journey, like most projects I have taken on, I am learning a whole lot.

For one, I am learning that most folks who aspire to start and run their own businesses underestimate the value of cultivating good relationships.

In fact, the lack of readiness by most entrepreneurs, especially those of color, is the biggest shocker (to me) during this process.

When we talk about "business relationships", it helps to try to zero-in on a) my definition of the term and b) to try to identify the categories of business relationships that if you are in business for yourself, you will encounter on a daily basis.

And how to best handle all these types of relationships in ways that places you and your firm in position to build a successful business.

People-powered

CHAPTER 5

HATERS AND FOOLS

In my view, all entrepreneurs will relate to their end users i.e., customers, clients, patients, etc. We also have other equally important business relationships to tend to as part of our day-to-day activities.

The typical story goes like this: You have an idea for some type of new service or product. In fact, you are so sure this new thing will change the world that you immediately tell some folks you know can help make this dream a reality.

Those folks get as excited as you are and as a result, you all decide to start a company around this idea.

Long story short, now you find yourself in a bit of a conundrum: Your product works, you have a few customers but now lack the funds you need to take things to the next level as they say.

You must go out and find folks who can understand your vision and see the economic potential in your idea. Whether you get funding from a bank, friends and family, or from professional investors, you will still have to have a long-term relationship, with at the very least, one kind of investor (as a startup seeking and receiving outside funding).

With these funds, at some point, as your business grows, you will probably hire your first set of employees.

In our little scenarios here, you are, as you continue to build your firm, having to create and manage various types of relationships.

All especially important relationships, might I add. The mistake I see most entrepreneurs make is that for some, these counterparties are just a means to an end. Some entrepreneurs approach the whole idea of investors as folks who are there to simply provide funding and nothing else.

In some personalities, ego and persecutory delusions start to take hold. Especially when things get tough in the business.

We often see some entrepreneurs who behave in a manner that suggests that they are on some journey (alone).

One that is often needlessly

interwoven into their sense of personal value. Once this mindset sets in, folks view anyone who offers critique or feedback as an enemy. The "I have a whole bunch of haters" mindset.

In my experience, speaking as a black man, I often see this type of behavior among people of color.

I am not sure why, we, in business often behave this way, but I do know that our reluctance to collaborate often leads to the widening of the wealth gap in our communities.

A global phenomenon of which "We" are seldom the beneficiaries.

As an entrepreneur, and I am sure you are, you must do your absolute best to clearly identify your business relationships and have a well thought out plan to nurture each.

It's just business...

In order to do so, we must try to understand a few things. First of all, business is just business. It is not about your standing in your community. It is not about your sense of self-worth. It really is not.

It is just business. And folks will get into business with you because they are looking for a return. They just want to make money. Afterall, that is what business (ultimately) is about, is it not?

The bank wants a return on the loan they give you and their main goal is to make sure that you, my friend, can pay back the loan plus interest.

This is the reason they keep asking you questions about your business. This is the reason for all these document requests.

Your business partners, well, hopefully they want to build wealth by helping grow the business. In the ideal situation, your business partners will all bring something of value to the proverbial table to help 10x the business you all are working so hard to build.

Your employees are looking to get a return for the time they put into your business.

Some employees are going to go the extra mile. They will bring all their talents to help you achieve exponential growth. They will be hard-working, smart, motivated, possess natural leadership skills, and so on. Granted, you will not come across this type of employee often, when you do, do not let them go unappreciated. I will get into this a bit later.

People-powered

CHAPTER 6

GLASS HOUSES

Here is the thing about one of the most elusive aspects of effective relationship management (in business).

As the proprietor of a small business, you will be faced with many challenges as you work to grow your organization.

At the heart of most obstacles will be

your ability, or not, to convince others to see the potential value in what you have to offer. Regardless of how you view each type of interaction.

You will have to get your customers to try your product or service, and perhaps, even continue to be patrons of your offerings.

You will need to inspire confidence in your employees on a daily basis.

Your partners will need to know that you are the right person to lead your organization. So will you investors.

Navigating these challenges will not be easy. And no matter the level of difficulty, no matter the circumstances, it is important to view each relationship as sacrosanct.

After all, your business will cease to exist without the funding you need from your investors, the loyalty of your customers, the support of your employees, and so on.

Customers

Your customers and/or clients will be and should be viewed as the lifeblood of your business. The most important group as far your business' long-term value goes.

I am serious. Whether you sell handbags or offer professional services, special attention paid to customer needs pays dividends eventually. Those to who you sell your goods are going to be the most important group of all.

Customer delineation

Depending on the type of business you have, and the size of your organization, like most dynamic enterprises, your firm will most likely have various types of customers.

This is just one of those things. Yes,

you will have various customer segments and personas. Sure. And each type of customer profile will have its own subsegments.

These types of customer breakdowns can be as straightforward or as complex as your business demands.

But for the sake of simplicity, let us consider the two types of customers being your Internal and External Customers.

Most small organizations make all the needed concessions and put in place various systems to navigate their relationships with their external customers.

Most tiny firms, however, often fail to truly address the needs of their internal customers.

What's the difference?

Well, for starters, your external customers are those that are most common and well known in business circles and beyond. These are the folks that literally and/or figuratively walk through the front door of your business to buy what you sell.

These are also your end users. That is if you are in the software space. These folks buy what you sell for personal or professional use.

Unlike these guys (your external customers), your internal customers can be folks in other departments within your organization. From the folks on the ground to the managing team of your company, anyone who works within your company can be considered an internal customer.

There are also those that are Connected Stakeholders of your business. These are folks who stand to benefit or be adversely affected by your business. The company that supplies your business with the raw materials needed to make your cupcakes can be considered a Connected Stakeholder. Your Investors are also Connected Stakeholders.

Of course, as I am sure you have figured out by now that some of these roles will overlap. The point is to a) keep in mind that each type of customer is equally important to the success of your organizations. And b) that Systems and processes should be created to nurture each of these types of relationships. We will dive a little deeper into the other types of customers and stakeholders a bit later.

People-powered

CHAPTER 7

CORPORATE COURTSHIP

With each party, each type of relationship comes various rules and processes one must adhere to. As businessfolk, it is often in our best interest, and the interest of the companies we operate, that we do what is necessary to ensure that our firms have all the components needed to function on a day-to-day basis and be profitable.

This is the number one priority every businessman, or woman must understand, internalize, and practice. We must often start with our customers. Folks today have many options when it comes to, well, everything.

In the world of consumer retail, or even banking, or entertainment - Folks have various brands to choose from when deciding where to spend their hard-earned cash. The same can be said for your investors as well.

Anyone with a little bit of cash (today) they wish to put to work, has various options.

With $0 commission trades and the option of equity crowdfunding, not to mention, cryptocurrencies, folks have various ways to earn money on their money, even more so than ever before. For this reason, I would highly recommend that you, as the business operator, do not take either party (customer or investor) for granted.

Brand origin story

Since folks have various different opportunities to buy stuff and/or invest their money, it is imperative that you start your relationship-building journey by first building your identity. Your corporate profile. Your brand story.

Besides selling coffee, which a dozen other shops (probably) do in your neighborhood, what will you be known for? How do you want folks to feel about your brand? What emotions do you want to elicit when folks do business with your company?

Successfully building your brand identity on a compelling story, one that reaches a specific group of customers (and investors) will go a long way to help set you apart from the competition.

2000 Western Avenue

Starbucks is a great example of a firm that has been able to do this very successfully. The fact that I do not have to explain what Starbucks is (to you), clearly illustrates the strength of the brand.

Now, you might be saying: "Hold on, but Starbucks is a huge coffee chain. Of course, it has a strong brand". And you are correct. But consider the fact that this huge international coffee chain started with one lonely store on 2000 Western Avenue in Seattle, WA.

With time and hard work (and cash), you too can build a world-famous brand.

It is important, however, that you know

from day one, what that identity will be, and who you will be looking to reach. In the world of direct sales, most new sales professionals start their careers by trying to reach "anyone".

It takes some time and experience for most of us in the arena to realize that we should spend most of our time and energy trying to reach "qualified" sales candidates only.

CHAPTER 8

BRAND EQUITY

As part of your brand identity brainstorming exercise, I would advise you to first consider your daily routines. We all have stuff we do on a daily basis. Shops and websites we visit frequently.

And it may come as no surprise to you that these daily activities, when looked at as a whole, say a lot about what type of person you are.

What type of shopper, business owner, etc. The things we repeatedly do gives anyone watching, an edge to trying to decode the puzzle that is you.

I go out for coffee every morning. And yes, I go to my local Starbucks. I am a Starbucks guy. But my wife prefers Dunkin. The thing is why we both like the coffee chains we like has nothing to do with the coffee. Of course, I found this out as a result of my frustration that when we go out to get coffee together, we have to go to two separate destinations. Anyway, I will not bore you with the details of our conversations.

Relevant brand value

What I will say is that I found out that she likes the fact that she can get in and out of any Dunkin' Donuts in less than three minutes. While a trip to Starbucks takes 15, sometimes 20 minutes.

She also likes the noncommittal taste of Dunkin coffee. Well, the description is my disdain for Dunkin showing. I, on the other hand, like Starbucks because I like to sit and enjoy the ambiance, the people, the community's goings and comings. Plus, I like the strong, punch you in the face taste of Starbucks coffee.

So, start with what you like and why you like what you like. Then try to understand the type of person you are. Consider the idea of what you are looking to offer in the marketplace, your competition, your story, and so on.

Love languages

As you move through your brand identity concepts, you will also want to devise a communication strategy. After all, this book is about building strong, healthy relationships with folks you do business with.

And we all know that communication is the foundation of every relationship. So, when telling your story, how will you tell it? Keep in mind that your brand will say a lot about your firm. The colors you choose to accentuate everything you offer, your tone, your communication channels, i.e., social media, radio spots on NPR, etc.

All of these must be considered carefully and be built around the type of folks you want to reach out to.

As you communicate with folks. Whether your initial messaging, while folks are in the process of doing business with your firm, or your communication after the fact, must be completely representative of the expectations you have – through your brand – set.

This part is vital to building brand trust and Goodwill. Your company will have various policies. You will share these policies on your website(s), mobile apps, and other branded surfaces. You will set expectations for almost every scenario.

Some will and must appear as part of your brand. As perhaps, your tagline.
Like *"When You're Here, You're Family"*, or *"The quicker picker-upper"*. Both of these tags set clear and measurable expectations.

I am sure you will be a bit pissed if the Olive Garden treated you like that help, although they promised to treat you like family, right? In its tag, the Italian cuisine chain has set an expectation. One the company must take extraordinary steps to make sure they reach each time.

And when they do not, there are policies and procedures in place to remedy whatever issue arises.

This is how you build strong relationships with your customers. Well, one of the ways. That is - setting expectations and following through on them.

Pennies and thoughts

When I was out here in these streets dating. Back in the good old days, before I got married (and saved), I found that when I listened more than I talked and took what my dates would tell me (about themselves) to build an experience for them, my dates went well.

Seeking, courting, and retaining customers works sort of like that. You must take every opportunity to interact with your customers.

You must make seeking feedback an integral part of your business practices. You must train all of your team members to take this very seriously.

History has taught us that companies that fail to listen to their customers and evolve as the needs of their customers change, fail.

In some instances, some brands go all the way with this concept. Some form *Customer advisory boards* to help advise the company on the ways in which it can better serve its customers. I wrote a book about this very topic: *"Customer Journeys: Why every Startup needs a Customer Advisory Board."*

Change Agents

It is important to take customer feedback and use said feedback to demonstrably improve the way your company does things. Once you do, as you do, you must take steps to communicate said changes with your customers, creating customer-centric stories around the inspiration for change.

Telling stories about specific aha moments brought on by specific customers. Telling these customer/change stories is a great way to lead into advocacy. Do not be afraid to stand for something.

Brands today are not only expected to sell stuff. Consumers want their brands to tell the world where they stand on various issues.

According to a recent survey conducted by the Corporate Social Mind, nearly 60% of Americans want the companies they buy products from to have a position about issues such as racial discrimination and social justice.

Roughly 50% of the survey's respondents (1,004) said they often do online research to see how a brand reacted to the social issues.

The same survey also found that over 45% of the respondents expressed their desire to see their favorite brands make public where they stand on the various issues.

Companies like McDonald's and Outback Steakhouse have been building stronger relationships with the communities they serve for years by taking a stand and being part of the kind of change they believe in.

"For some reason founders get their ego

involved in fundraising where it's a personal victory. It is the tiniest step on the way..."

- *Ron Conway*

CHAPTER 9

IT'S COMPLICATED

Entrepreneurs everywhere - from New York to Nairobi - (often) harbor mixed feelings about their investors. These feelings sometimes veer into the adversarial when there are disagreements about the future of the underlying firm, or firms.

Often when things are not going well. Ahem! NO PROFITS. That is when folks bump heads the most.

To be fair, your relationship with the folks who bet their hard-earned money on the future success of your organization will be one of the most complicated ones you will ever have.

There are many reasons why these types of bonds come with a huge side of complications. Reasons from the workable to the insurmountable. The scenarios that I often come across revolve around this idea that, from the entrepreneur's perspective, the investor somehow "doesn't get it".

And that both parties, in instances where differences of opinion may exist, do not want the same things, as far as the relevant corporate entity is concerned.

Truth be told, there is no greater vote of confidence, no louder thumbs up, than one expressed via cash.

Regardless of the reasons for any anxiety, and/or animosity, it is in all parties' best interest that the investor-entrepreneur relationship remains civil and, most importantly, profitable.

Capital (gains)

The business of money. One has to place themselves in the shoes of those who operate companies that have money as their product. For these men and women, cash is the tool they use to make more cash.

Like Kevin O'leary from NBC's Shark Tank says, *"I like to send my money out in hopes that they return with friends"*. I am paraphrasing of course. This is the world in which most, if not all professional investors live.

For any entrepreneur, passionate about their own business, and all the ins and outs of said business, this reality is difficult to fathom.

This disconnect often results in friction in our relationship with our investors.

Whether we have Venture capitalists or Angel investors as our initial investors, we must understand the need for these types of partners to obsess over profitability.

The quest for short-term profits must not be seen by you or any other folks on your startup team as a bad thing. You must understand that it is never ideal for a business, regardless of your future plans to go for too long without bringing home the bacon. Or at the very least having the mechanisms needed in place to allow profits to roll in (at any time).

This is a fact that most seasoned investors understand. This fact often clashes with the ideals of most entrepreneurs who at any given time, believe that short term profits is fair game to be sacrificed for long-term value.

Both parties are not wrong here. The idea is to find a medium and communicate clearly what both sides want with plans to get there.

It is therefore vital that we, as entrepreneurs, craft our communications with our investors to adequately address this issue. Taking an adversarial position against your investors based on this material difference is never ideal.

People-powered

CHAPTER 10

MARRIAGE BOOT CAMP

I am no Psychotherapist, but I can tell you that one of the reasons why relationships, any relationship fails is because those involved lose sight of what is important and as a result fail to nurture and manage the most fundamental elements of what makes said relationship work.

We start to forget why we got together in the first place. And even when we try and fail to keep our bonds strong, we seldom communicate with one another and fail to take the extra steps to get things back on track.

As founders, our relationships with our investors, partners and employees follow patterns not unlike any other human-to-human relationships we have. Though each type a little different, there are some major commonalities present in what makes each type of relationship work.

Successful first dates

Things often start out well but can take a

dark turn as our relationship(s) progress. Ask any professional investor, and based on their response, you will be able to deduce that more often than not, the major culprit behind the demise of most business deals/relationships is the death of the underlying relationship itself.

More so than the lack of funding, unmet market demand, lack of product-market fit, or any of the reasons one might think would cause the dissolution of any corporate entity.

In other words, the inability of folks to continue to work together has taken down more promising businesses than you might think.

Narcissus and Echo

For us to try to understand and adopt tools to help manage any business relationship, new or old, particularly one with those who have invested in our organizations, we must try to uncover some of the reasons why these vital relationships can devolve.

We must first try to understand what it is we are doing. Let me elaborate. Whether you are in the process of seeking outside investment/investors for your company, or you currently have a growing number of investors, we must first try to understand our place – as entrepreneurs/founders - in these types of arrangements.

You, my friend, are just one of many startup founders out there. Many other men and women have great ideas too.
Most, much more innovative than yours. You are merely there to serve as the key to the provision of quality goods and services to your customers, stable paychecks and valuable stock options to your employees, and profits for your shareholders.

You, if you retain ownership in your firm, are just one of many owners of THE organization. These statements must be internalized as a way to check your ego.

Some folks suffer not from this all-too-common application. Those are the lucky few. For the rest of us, we must endure the side effects of growing up in a world that even Narcissus himself could not have imagined.

I have met many entrepreneurs whose sense of self-importance, though they wouldn't admit it, trumps their desire to see their companies succeed. One of the major issues of adopting a narcissistic view of the world, as any mental health professional will tell you, is that you fail to empathize.

You often neglect to prioritize, even process the needs, wants, and feelings of those around you.

When it comes to the way you manage your relationship with your investors, this cannot be the case if you are to build a successful organization.

Especially if you are typically the one seeking funding and not the one doing the funding.

Narcissus *gazing at his own reflection. The Greek*

mythological inspiration for the term Narcissist

CHAPTER 11

MOVING TARGETS

We, humans, possess many natural skills. Traits we somehow inherited from our ancestors. The natural talent for trade, in my view, is one of those traits that folks from all backgrounds, all cultures shares.

Acquiring or making something for x amount of time and resources and exchanging the finished product or service for $x + y$ (dollars) or something else of greater value is a practice our species has been engaged in since the dawn of time.

Try giving a child $3 for a toy their parent paid $4 for, and their reluctance to make this trade will help you notice that even a two-year-old knows this is not a fair trade.

Being in the unenviable position to helm a new company comes with many moving targets.

AT the heart of this sea of changing circumstances and challenges, comes the goal of profitability.

Money in the bank

Most folks who give you their hard cold cash to go out and build your business are betting that you and your team can reach this goal.

And this goal, this milestone, is more

elusive than you might think.

Did you know that most public companies make no money? And by "no money", I mean they are unprofitable. That is correct.

I know it does not seem like it. I mean with all the talks of cap tables and billion-dollar valuations, you might think folks are out here making money all willy-nilly.
The truth is, these astronomical valuations are derived from folks betting these firms will eventually make money. Most "Unicorns" are so because Investors hope they become so, down the line.

Most of these trendy startups languish for years burning through cash and borrowing from Peter to pay Paul. Paul, the guy from the I.T department.

He requires a paycheck regardless of whether or not the startup he works for has money in the bank.

In fact, only about 30 – 40% of U.S publicly-traded firms are profitable.

Long-term value
I say all this to say that, as a company, you offer your investors, partners, and employees the greatest value if and when you reach profitability.

Most Venture capital professionals advise that startup founders bootstrap for as long as they can. And if you are able to present your firm to outside investors showing profits, you will be in the best position possible to extract the highest value for your organization.

This is the reason, well, one of the reasons why as investors, we were all excited about the recent Coinbase IPO.

The San Francisco, California-based

Cryptocurrency platform so far has been one of the few tech startups to go public as a profitable company.

Of course, we know that this is but a dream. This is a feat few startups can claim during the first five years of their existence. Amazon, the online retail giant, was unprofitable for a long time. Even today, the company enjoys net margins of only about 5% annually.

In reality, you will have to plan your business in such a way that allows for, and clearly communicates your plan for profitability.

Great expectations

These plans are often expressed in your business plan, pitch decks, and any other documents you use to communicate your vision to potential investors.

I think almost all entrepreneurs who

are serious about building their businesses create concise plans not just for profitability, but one that has all the milestones and estimated timelines for these milestones to be reached, you and your team's ability to reach these milestones, and so forth.

In my experience, things tend to go wrong down the line when clear lines of communication are not established at the outset of the entrepreneur-investor relationship. Folks, the folks you talk to and look to have this type of relationship with, must know what the plan is.

We can also create problems with said investors when we go out and do things that were not expressed in those initial documents without first communicating any change in plans with those who exchanged their money for a piece of your company.

It is kind of like marriage. There are

typically three types of problems that can ruin a marriage:

1) folks change their minds about what they want and fail to communicate these changes with their partner.

2) Folks are not honest about who they are, what they want, etc. during the dating phase of the relationship and 3) something unexpected happens that both parties fail to navigate as a team.

It is imperative that you create a harmonious, cordial, even affectionate relationship with your investors.

Most can wait for profits. That is what they do. They are early-stage investors, remember? We just must do a better job and be real when starting off the relationship.

People-powered

CHAPTER 12

GROWING PAINS

As you grow your business, constant contact with your investors will become a challenge. This is natural. It is easy to jump on the phone with investors if you only have a handful of them, and if your company is still small.

Recent changes in the JOBS Act. allows for entrepreneurs to raise up to $5,000,000 in crowd equity funding, as compared to the previous $1 million annual limit.

What this means for you, the entrepreneurs, is that you can suddenly find yourself in a situation where you are dealing with hundreds, even thousands of investors.

I see this all the time in the startup world. As you pick up more investors, more customers, more employees, maintaining healthy, open lines of communications with your investors becomes a challenge.

Your investors will have questions. They will want some one-on-one time with you. No matter how small their investment is, your attitude cannot, and should not be that of the guy (or gal) who only has time for the high-dollar investors.

You do not need me to tell you that

this approach is wrong on many levels. Not to mention potentially legally perilous.

Investor relations

What you want to do is create systems to address this issue. Create dates and times when you hold virtual Q&As with your investors.

There are two ways I have seen this type of system work well. Some folks try to build deeper bonds with their investors and share with them various milestones the company has reached via in-person, event-type activities.

Apple, the iPhone maker, is known for holding these grand presentation-style events. A tradition started by the late Steve Jobs.

He, Jobs, would use these opportunities to cover various topics, including the introduction of new products. These need not replace the mandated general annual meetings, or quarterly reports.

Warren and Charlie

No! Rather, these types of events can give your investors a great opportunity to get some quality facetime with you and your team.

Not to be outdone, Warren Buffett, for his conglomerate, Berkshire Hathaway, also holds annual events for its investors. Except, in the case of Berkshire, these events are less presentation-y, and more like the county fair.

Like in most of these types of cases, investors in Berkshire get to touch and feel the products they have invested in and also to ask Warren, and Charlie a whole host of questions.

Since Warren rarely sits for interviews, the press and the rest of the financial world, get to peer into the minds of these two highly consequential men as a result of remarks delivered at these events.

Warren also goes out of his way to pen a personal shareholder letter each year. In these letters, as you would expect, he covers the status of the firm, the state of the global economy, as well as many other topics.

You can feel free to draw inspiration from these two examples as a way to communicate with your investors in a morale-boosting way.

Warren Buffett *tossing a newspaper at the Berkshire Hathaway annual shareholders meeting in Omaha in 2015.*

Landing pages

I find it helpful to create a page on your startup company's website that is password protected. You can share login credentials with your investors. Wix, the popular DIY web design platform has the tools needed to do this.

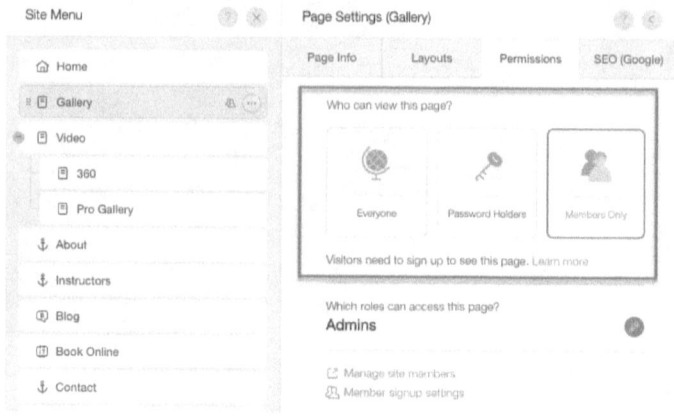

On this members-only page, you can share all documents, the answers to all frequent questions, updates, financials, etc.

I have found that building these systems helps constantly communicate where you are in your journey to building a profitable business. This also helps keep your investors less anxious.

"The greatest leader is not necessarily the one who does the greatest things. He is the one that gets the people to do the greatest things."

--Ronald Reagan

People-powered

CHAPTER 13

SPORTS METAPHORS

Contrary to what most people might think, great companies are not built around great products and/or services. Sure, it definitely helps to have a superior product, or two, out there on the market.

It sure as heck does not hurt to have the resources to build great marketing campaigns to help promote said products and services.

The kind of messaging that helps connect with your ideal potential customers in ways that clearly educates them on the all the advantages of using your product. Those are great too.

But *people* are the key to building great companies. For real. In fact, great people make great companies.

That being said, it is of the utmost importance that the members of your startup team, from partners to employees, are chosen carefully.

It is important, for the sake of the future of your firm, that you go into business, at the outset, with folks you genuinely like.

The kind of folks that you get along with and can cultivate healthy working relationships with.

Ever seen a couple that does business together? What usually happens if they divorce? The company often falls apart, right? What changed? Their relationship. That's what.

It is super important that your team works well together. Working with the kind of folks you can feel comfortable inviting over to your house for beers is more important than you might think.

Kind of like how you can tell that LeBron James actually likes the guys on his team.

Band of brothers

Some say teammates on professional sports teams often form bonds that are sometimes stronger than those they share with even their spouses.

I say all this to drive home the point that it is crucial to build your firm with folks you like.

Now don't get me wrong. I am by no means suggesting that you simply go into business with your friends. That would be irresponsible.

I am not asking that you make admission to your team solely based on likeability or friendship. You want to assemble a team of folks who are qualified and have various backgrounds relevant to delivering on your vison. That's for sure.

I am suggesting that these qualified folks be the kind of folks you can build health working relationships with.

The type that you can work with through all the challenges that are sure to come your way.

Conduct unbecoming.
One of the most pressing issues you must keep at the forefront of your recruiting practices is the idea that a team that plays well together wins.

You must keep this mantra, above most, when looking for folks to join your startup team.

Sure, talent, experience, expertise, these are all great when building a startup team. However, above all else must be your crew's ability to get along and work well together.

I don't wish to sound naive in proposing that yours, or any startup environment for that matter, be totally free of conflict.

I am aware that this is not humanly possible. No matter the company, or no matter how well your people get along, or that you get along with your folks, there are going to be instances of conflict and even confrontation.

It takes a whole lot of passion to build a company. And sometimes, this passion can come out in ways unbecoming of an evolved human.

This is a merely a natural consequence of the human condition. You, however, only want to, for the sake of your business and your own sanity, entertain the good kind of conflict.

Difference in opinion about the future of your organization. Skirmishes about product design, marketing budgets, and so on. These types of disagreements, as long as they don't result in less-than-civil behavior, are good types of conflict.

What you do not want is to assemble a team with chronic interpersonal dissension. This can lead to the slow and painful death of your company. Not to mention, the disenchantment of a lot of concerned stakeholders.

Growing your team from a small group of friends and associates to a full-blown company, while maintaining a productive, purposeful work environment is ideal.

So, how can one accomplish, or begin to negotiate such a seemingly impossible feat?

Well, it depends on a number of important factors. All of which must revolve around the type of person (or persons) you ask to join your startup team. At the outset, you needn't worry too much about putting together a congenial team.

Since most of the early folks you bring on will most likely be folks you already know, you will know whether or not these folks, including yourself, can build a profitable, people-powered business and have fun while you do so.

As time goes on, however, and your team goes from just a few guys and gals to 10, 14, or more folks, you will need to create some sort of multidimensional, multifaceted system that helps you attract and retain folks who fit into your company culture.

As you transition from the "brand-new startup" phase into a real company, you will be able to tap into your resources and leverage your human capital to build these aforementioned robust recruiting systems.

One frequently used hack, however, is to ask the folks on your team to recommend some of their associates for employment. This is one surefire way to ensure that those on your initial team stay on task and are not distracted by drama.

Folks will ask other folks they like and know are qualified to join your team. Folks will want to come into the office simply because they will spend their days surrounded by other folks they like and therefore work well with.

CHAPTER 14

CORNER OFFICES

Just as on any other type of team, in any other scenario, the guys and gals on your startup team must each play a specific position, or two.

Look, I understand that in the case of a young company, the order of the day is more *"all-hands-on-deck"* than specifically designated positions/roles.

Heck, in most cases, you will be the only team member. As in, your startup just has you and no other employees. The solopreneur kind of situation.

I get that this might be the case for

you. In which case, these words, this book, might serve as (just) a guide to help you navigate future potentially cantankerous situations. But all things being equal, you will want to, as I mentioned, recruit and retain folks based on their abilities. Specifically, the kind of abilities that will add value to your business.

Flat Earth 'Theory'

If you are among the lucky few who can access folks with whom you share similar passions, and a desire to build a business, and also possess the talent and skill to build said business, it is important that you capitalize on your unique advantageous position.

It is crucial that detailed discussions are had. And roles are equitably disseminated. It is also important that a basic corporate structure is established.

Regardless of the origins of folks' relationships prior to working together, lines and processes need to be established.

I honestly do not feel that it is my place to point you in the direction of any particular corporate/management structure.

Which one you choose will be mostly in response to the needs of your business and your personal style, of course.

Some, in the software space favor the flat management structure over your traditional hierarchical corporate setups.

Be that as it may, it is absolutely imperative that lines are drawn and an appreciation for sad lines line up as one of the requirements of admission to the team. Roles will need to be recognized and respected by all.

This is one of the major ways in which you can ensure that your team, while ringing the cash registers, remains respectful and loving towards one another.

Cultural studies

Equally as important as the whole idea of having well-defined roles for various members of your team, and having a well-defined corporate structure is your corporate culture.

The thing about the modern corporate landscape, I mean with all the information available to investors and the general public about the firms we all watch, we all have some kind of idea what many of our favorite brands, and the people behind them get up to, right?

We all are well aware that while outfits like Goldman maintain a more serious, traditional work environment, companies like Red Ventures, the sales-oriented, privately owned Charlotte, NC-based firm prefers a more relaxed, frat house kind of atmosphere.

For the most part, your corporate culture will fall into place, (over time) naturally. I ask only that you remain proactive and vigilant in your quest to help shape just what type of outfit you want to run, as far as culture is concerned.

CHAPTER 15

CLAN ADHOCRACY

Thanks to a global social awakening, including both the murder of George Floyd and the #metoo movement, people from all walks of life are having to address what it means to live in a fair and equitable world.

A world free of sexual harassment, police brutality, poverty, and disease.

Corporate leaders and politicians alike are faced with the task of redefining the modern workplace environment and the laws needed to govern a much-needed panorama of meaningful social change.

In 2020, COVID-19 helped drive this

conversation into areas no one thought possible. We are now all, as a global community, wondering what it means for one to "go to work", or to "work". What it means to have police presence on the streets of cities and towns all across the world. What it means to be an investor. And what it means to have money.

George Perry Floyd Jr. was an African American man murdered by police during an arrest after a store clerk alleged, he had passed a counterfeit $20 bill in Minneapolis.

Interspecies consonance

As a result of all these seismic shifts, company leaders are now forced take vital steps to re-define their company cultures.

At the vanguard of this multipronged global movement are folks like you, the entrepreneurs.

You are in a great position to take all the ingredients the current world order has to offer and build a business that is well-positioned to take on the challenges of the 21st century.

Among, the many issues you are forced to address is your ability to craft a business that is open to folks from all walks of life.

One that is able to, while creating

great products and services, also create a culturally diverse, and safe work environment for your people, and the entire community you serve.

That being said, there are many ways and various avenues one such as yourself can explore in your quest to foster positive business/work relationships. First, between you and all those you do business with, and among the members of your team.

With every word so far (in this book), I have made an honest attempt to stress to you how important it is in business, at every level, to maintain positive, productive relationships with your fellow humans. One demarcated by humility, patience, and understanding.

Not only is this the right and healthy thing to do, keep in mind that positivity leads to productivity. Productivity begets profitability. And isn't that the whole point of business?

Grand gestures

A natural extension of that reality is often reflected in the kind of workplace you will create, are creating, or have built thus far. Believe it or not, your team will follow your lead. Eventually, your workplace, your office, the culture your team perpetuates and shares, will be a macrocosm of your personality.

I too, at some point in my career, inadvertently built a highly toxic work environment. An environment in which everyone was at each other's throats all the time.

One in which I, for some strange reason, thought pitting members of my team against one another would lead to productivity. It did not. In fact, the opposite happened.

There was so much sadness in the air all the time. Most of the great men and women I worked with left in epically bad ways. The ones who stayed either hated me, themselves, or both.

I pretended for a while that this was all someone else's fault. At some point though I had to face myself and the monster I had created.

Needless to say, I had to dig deep to find out why I acted this way. With lots of help and soul searching, I started to undo some of the damage I had done.

I had to retrain my mind to understand that we, my team, myself, we were all just parts of one unit.

I had to breakdown the internally competitive ecosystem I had created and foster collaboration instead. Bonds needed to be built, not walls and barriers.

CHAPTER 16

COMMUNITY EQUITY

One sure way to help build these bonds is by consciously and purposefully building a diverse team/workplace. This is as important a topic as any other.

You want to infuse diversity into your organization in every way imaginable. Not only will these actions help create a well-balanced work environment, but diversity will also help make your company a smarter, more productive organization.

For real. According to a Harvard Business Review survey of 1700 companies across eight countries (the U.S., France, Germany, China, Brazil, India, Switzerland, and Austria), Companies that are more diverse than average had 19% higher innovation revenues in 2018. Based on results from this survey, in the same year, 43 % of firms with diverse boards saw higher profits.

Companies that are ethnically diverse are 35% more likely to achieve above-average financial returns. Diverse teams are 87% better at decision-making.

All these "higher than average" figures lead to higher-than-average profits. And remember, that is the point of being in business, right?

Cambrian explosion

As you can see, fostering diversity is not only great for building lasting bonds among your team but also great for the bottom line.

Adopting and enforcing a diversity and inclusion strategy as part of your overall business agenda goes beyond simply hiring and/or working with a diverse group of people.

No ma'am. The "big picture" of your business needs must be at the top of your mind while you seek to create a more diverse and inclusive organization.

Not to be confused with diversity, inclusivity fosters equal access to opportunities within your organization that would be typically reserved for those in the majority, or an arbitrarily select few.

Equal access to career advancement paths, ownership programs, work-related travel, advanced training opportunities, etc. These can all be the building blocks of your inclusivity initiatives.

One can even go as far as to build a work environment in which creative mentorship programs are part of the onboarding/training process.

Pairing folks who would otherwise have never interacted with one another within the organization to take on various projects.

Pairing up the heads of marketing with the guys and gals in the graphic design department to work hand-in-hand on some new marketing project.

You can build greater bonds between those with who you work by helping create peer support groups within your organization to address a host of issues.

I find that these types of programs are most helpful in helping folks within the organization address sensitive issues.

Creating peer support groups within your organization can also help spark various innovative ways in which your company can address complex challenges both within and outside of your company.

Sometimes, as entrepreneurs/CEOs, we tend to be so focused on building our businesses that we miss great opportunities right in front of us.

Some of these opportunities can arise out of a need to solve some issue among your ranks. Some basic deductive reasoning, an extrapolation here and there, and voila! The firm has a new product or service.

One born out of solutions you create to be used internally.

You can encourage off-site, or non-work-related social interactions/events between you and members of your team. Those, when conducted properly, always help folks get to know one another and help foster greater connections among folks within your firm.

Your company can also truly benefit by creating s robust reward system in which all folks, from all levels of your organization, can share in the overall ownership of your company.

International travel when available should be extended to folks from all corners of your organization. Your diversity plans should not be executed as just some cosmetic, goodwill-hunting expedition.

You should consider your plans for your firm while you seek to execute some of these steps. For one, you will want to consider your customer base. For example,

just for the sake of your bottom line, you will not want to staff your plus size women's clothing distribution operation with a bunch of white dudes, now, would you?

In the end, the whole point of taking some of these steps discussed here in this hopefully, interesting, best-selling book – ok, I know I am pushing it – is to provide you with some sort of basic guide to use to build stronger, more positive bonds with the folks you work with and do business with. I hope you have enjoyed these mindless rants.

"None of us, including me, ever do great things. But we can all do small things,

with great love, and together we can do something wonderful."

– Mother Teresa

CHAPTER 17

IT TAKES A VILLAGE

It takes a village. Not just to raise a child, but, in my opinion, to get just about anything of import accomplished.

The wise ones among us. The village elders. The ones whose eyes have seen more of this world than the rest of us. Those who know better.

This old African proverb/mantra has been the prevailing wisdom among my people, the Ashantis, for as long as anyone can remember.

This idea has also evidently been adopted and internalized by various other cultures around the world today.

In 2006, former first lady Hillary Rodham Clinton wrote a riveting book (It Takes a Village) about this very idea.

In her best-selling book, the 2016 presidential candidate and former New York State Senator, talked about the importance of creating a society that enables children to become smart, able, resilient adults.

This very concept. This simple but powerful proposition has been used to help stress the importance of collaboration along many, many lines and aspects of human life.

From those who hail from the far east to modern day Europe, to Africa and everywhere in between.

We all know, on some subconscious level, that we must set aside our differences if we are to accomplish great things.

In most corners of the world, especially in developed nations, kids are taught to think and operate this way from an early age.

The economies and educational structures of the top ten most advanced nations are built to encourage, foster, and reward teamwork/collaboration.

The most popular types of sports are ones based on the hard work of a group of like-minded, skilled, men and women working together to bring home the gold.

We are pack animals. We do not

always like to admit it, but we are. This realization and the consequences of being denied one's pack is even more evident during these trying (COVID-19) times.

Even as kids, we were at our best when working and playing with other kids. Children know, on a natural level, to help one another.

This is who we are. It is in our DNA. We are built to work, play, grow, and live together.

Our prehistoric ancestors did it. How else would they have stood a chance against the Woolly mammoth or the Saber-toothed tiger? Or any other wild beast they were forced to fight off, or hunt for food and clothing.

Even as humans transitioned from a Hunter-gatherer species to other forms of sustainable food supply and economic systems, we did so as a group at first.

Then, later into various separate groups that farmed and traded with one another.

It is a well-known fact that citizenship to ancient Rome was a matter of geography/record, and not a question of ethnic identity. A practice carried out till today by most nations.

The great Persian empire consisted of

folks from all ends of the ethnic, religious, and continental spectrum. Her armies were manned by Africans, Asians, and even Greeks. This is what made her such an enduring force.

I preach not warfare, of course. Only that great things get done when we work with others regardless of shared identities.

In business, one must understand and make this a guiding force as you seek to transact with other humans.

You must let your better angels guide you. You must remain humble, open-minded, patient, and kind. Then and only then will you be able to build something great and profitable.

People-powered

Thank you!

Thank you so much for giving me a chance to be part of your literary/educational diet.

I try to put out books that I think will help provide value to others about various topics that I tell myself I have gained some insight into – or, at the very least, have some experience with.

I often get feedback about the books I, and my publisher, put out. I then use this feedback to improve, and at times, completely change the way I write and/or the topics I write about.

We, and by (we), I mean all of us here at OSTRICH find such feedback extremely useful as we try to carry out our mission to create engaging content.

That being said, please feel free to log onto www.ostrichpress.com or visit our Amazon, Kobo, and Google Play pages to let us know what you think about this book, and any others (from us) you may have read.

And once again, Thank you!

People-powered

NOTES

https://en.wikipedia.org/wiki/How_to_Win_Friends_and_Influence_People

https://en.wikipedia.org/wiki/Dale_Carnegie

https://quotesgram.com/img/dale-carnegie-quotes-business/474985/

https://smallbiztrends.com/2015/06/build-lasting-business-relationships.html

https://news.gallup.com/opinion/gallup/266927/americans-perceptions-success.aspx

https://smallbiztrends.com/2011/12/top-one-percent-own-businesses.html

https://www.forbes.com/sites/elainepofeldt/2020/05/30/survey-nearly-30-of-americans-are-self-employed/?sh=29b3b55b2d21

https://www.forbes.com/sites/thesba/2013/08/02/7-steps-for-dealing-with-angry-customers/?sh=74ee1cdc6d27

https://www.sciencedirect.com/topics/engin

eering/external-customer#:~:text=External%20Customers&text=These%20are%20the%20people%20or,illustrated%20by%20a%20few%20examples%3A&text=A%20person%20buys%20a%20car,the%20new%20car%20dealer's%20customer).

https://en.wikipedia.org/wiki/Starbucks#History

https://www.thecorporatesocialmind.com/researchusa

https://medium.com/how-to-start-a-startup/17-quotes-from-marc-andreessen-ron-conway-on-how-to-raise-money-d0b710f115f1#:~:text=%E2%80%9CYou're%20almost%20always%20better,and%20I%20think%20that's%20true%E2%80%9D

https://www.greekboston.com/culture/mythology/narcissus-echo/

https://fortune.com/2016/04/28/warren-buffett-berkshire-annual-meeting-omaha/

https://hrdailyadvisor.blr.com/2018/04/12/4-distinct-types-corporate-culture/

https://sharemylesson.com/blog/death-of-george-floyd

https://en.wikipedia.org/wiki/George_Floyd

https://www.dictionary.com/browse/vanguard

https://hbr.org/2018/01/how-and-where-diversity-drives-financial-performance

https://www.lexico.com/en/definition/inclusivity

https://www.forbes.com/sites/janicegassam/2019/02/04/diversity-without-inclusion-is-useless/?sh=7a906c2a5685

https://www.nami.org/Blogs/NAMI-Blog/August-2018-/Peer-Support-Helping-Others-Healing-Yourself#:~:text=A%20peer%20support%20group%20is,their%20experiences%2C%20struggles%20and%20challenges.

https://blog.hubspot.com/marketing/teamwork-quotes

https://www.amazon.com/Takes-Village-

Hillary-Rodham-Clinton-ebook/dp/B000N0WTC4

https://www.simonandschuster.com/books/It-Takes-a-Village/Hillary-Rodham-Clinton/9781416540649

ABOUT THE AUTHOR

Frank is a serial entrepreneur, author and investor. Frank has written various books on topics like Marketing, social media, entrepreneurship and other areas of business. He resides in Charlotte, North Carolina with his business partner/wife, Bernice.

People-powered

People-powered

RECOMMENDED READING

Customer Journeys: Why every Startup needs a Customer Advisory Board.

What happens when you listen to your customers? What happens when you build a customer-centric startup? - One that is intricately connected to its customers and all the men and women whose lives are impacted every day by your products and services?

STATUS UPDATE

Strategic social media marketing can be the cure-all your business needs to reach the right audience at the right time. STATUS UPDATE is an easy-to-digest guide to help any Life and/or Health agent or agency make the most of their Facebook marketing system.

'STATUS UPDATE' is a must-read for any Insurance Agency owner or Broker looking for unique ideas on how to get the most out of their Facebook marketing - Gathoni Njenga

STATUS UPDATE

How to generate and convert health and life insurance sales leads with Facebook Ads

FRANK DAPPAH

Small business social media marketing guide

CONTINUOUS CONNECTIVITY: Leveraging the power of text messaging to grow your business and enhance your brand reach.

I have always considered Sales and Marketing to be that which is most vital to the Startup success and growth of any organization - both at the for profit and nonprofit level. You can have the best ice cream, or coffee in town.

Find these and many other titles from the author at Amazon.com, Ostrichpress.com, or wherever you buy books.

People-powered

OSTRICH®

Ostrich Publishers

We love books! It is in our DNA. It is the food we eat and the air we breathe.

We are working hard to build an all-inclusive publishing and distribution platform.

Our Mission

OSTRICH is an all-digital publisher. Our mission is to create a robust medium through which talented independent Authors and Creatives can share their works with the rest of the world.

What We Do

As part of our overall mission, we work closely with authors of all backgrounds to help bring their works to life. Through our robust distribution infrastructure, we can help Authors, who would otherwise go unnoticed, to plan, create and distribute their finished products worldwide. We work with Authors at every step of the process, from brainstorming, to writing, to distribution and marketing. We are working hard to build an all-inclusive publishing and distribution platform.

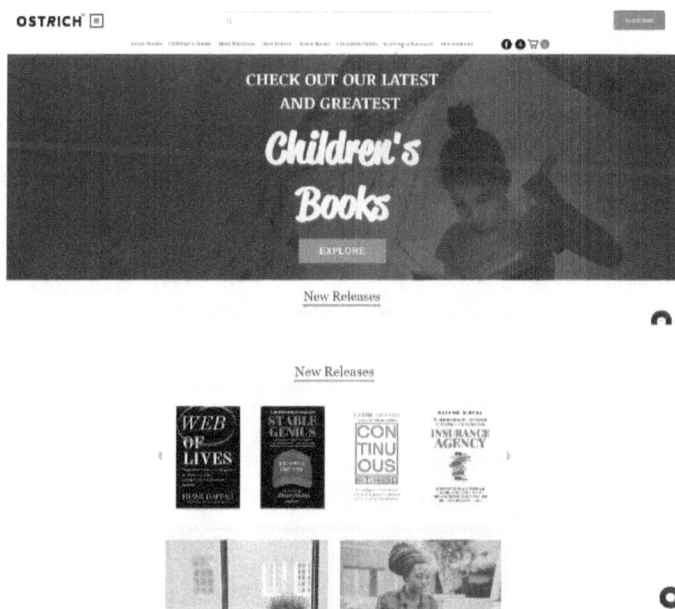

OSTRICH Publishers (https://www.ostrichpress.com/)

People-powered

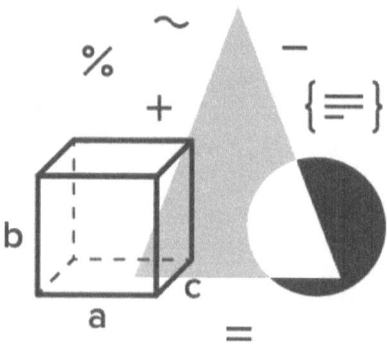

Copyright © 2012 Ostrich press

All rights reserved.

ISBN: 9798742845836

PEOPLE-POWERED

The road to success and happiness cuts right through (the quality of) our relationships with others.

Our relationship with our fellow humans is the most important aspect of our lives.

Try as we (sometimes) might, we keep coming back to the same reality: We are all stuck together on this beautiful blue planet we call home.

It is then more urgent then ever, to make the effort, as a group, to nurture our bonds with those we interact with the most.

OSTRICH
OSTRICH PUBLISHERS
MADE IN THE U.S.A
WWW.OSTRICHPRESS.COM

People-powered

People-powered

www.ingramcontent.com/pod-product-compliance
Lightning Source LLC
Chambersburg PA
CBHW031631210526
45464CB00004B/1850